PRESENTED TO

Nita

FROM

Robyn

DATE

July, 2006

Nothing can separate you from the love of God.
Thank you for being the wonderful person God created.

BEAUTIFULLY PINNED PROMISES

Blessings from God in the Book of Psalms

mary grace birkhead

Design by Brand Navigation
Bill Chiaravalle, DeAnna Pierce,
Russ McIntosh & Brittany Gerwig

INTEGRITY®
PUBLISHERS
Nashville

THIS BOOK IS DEDICATED TO MY SISTERS,

DEDE CAVAZOS & MELISSA OVERMYER.

THE OLDER WE GET THE MORE PRECIOUS YOU BECOME!

I LOVE YOU.

Thank you to my husband, Rob, who picks up the loose ends of my life and makes writing possible. To my dear children, Robert, Daniel, and Camille, who love and serve others so beautifully. To the people who encourage me with God's Word: Mary Birkhead, Rhonda Levitch, Tonya Chalfant, Kathy Dalton, Julie Meier (who has great courage), Brenda Schulte, Joanna Cranford, Susan Lipson, Julie Ward, and Carol Virden. My pastors, Lloyd Shadrach and Jeff Schulte. To the brave people at Integrity Publishers for believing in these books: Byron Williamson, Mark Gilroy, Barb James, Betty Woodmancy, Dale Wilstermann, and Joey Paul. And special thanks to Bill Chiaravalle, DeAnna Pierce, Russ McIntosh, and Brittany Gerwig for making this book so beautiful.

INTRODUCTION

One of my favorite things as a little girl was rummaging through my mother's jewelry drawer. My two sisters and I loved to put on her pins, earrings, and necklaces. Some of the jewelry was just scattered in the drawer. Some special things were kept in little leather boxes. But her most beautiful pins were protected in a tin box with a picture of the Queen of England on it. I remember being mesmerized by the picture of the young queen and her beautiful jewels. In my mind, my mother's jewelry was almost as impressive. We would dress up and pretend we were fancy ladies having tea. Sometimes we were brides or queens. And because we had no brothers, occasionally I was forced to be the prince!

The Book of Psalms is like going through one of God's jewelry boxes. Psalms is a picture of all human emotions—from sadness, anger, fear, longing, and confusion to praying, resting, rejoicing, singing, and laughing. Psalms is truly a passionate book. *Beautifully Pinned Promises* identifies some of the blessings of God you don't want to miss. He has jewels for us to hold on to and call our own.

This is a book for you. The truth in it is yours. Yes, the words are old, but the promises are eternally yours. We forget many things as we grow up. If you grew up going to church, you may have forgotten the wisdom and rest that was promised to you. If you didn't go to church as a child, you might not know that there are sixty-six jewelry boxes (books of the Bible!) for you to go through and discover the riches. You'll feel like you are the girl on the tin box. But even better, you'll know that you are the daughter of the King of Kings!

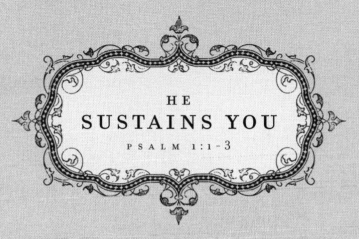

HE
SUSTAINS YOU
PSALM 1:1-3

You are like a tree planted
by streams of water, which yields its fruit in season and
whose leaf does not wither. Whatever you do prospers.

You are filled with God's power as you
stay close to Him. He will empower
you to live a miraculous life. All things happen
in His time, which is perfect!
Keep your roots by His stream and let
Him produce fruit in your life.

HE
SEES YOU
PSALM 1:6A

For the Lord
watches over the way of the righteous.

He never blinks or misses a thing.
You are in His grasp and protection. He is over
all things and all people.
He is actively working at all times.
Wait and trust in Him!

HE SURROUNDS
YOU

PSALM 2:12B

Blessed are all
that take refuge in Him.

He welcomes you. His arms are open.
His mercy and love for you are endless.
You can rest in His powerful
and safe presence.
You can hide in Him
and let Him take your fear away.

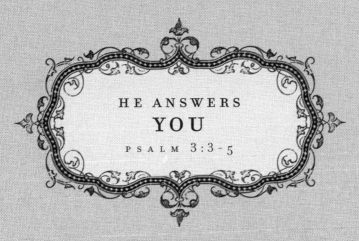

HE ANSWERS
YOU
PSALM 3:3-5

But you are a shield around me,
O Lord, You bestow glory on me and lift up my head.
To the Lord I cry aloud, and He answers me from
His holy hill. I lie down and sleep; I wake again,
because the Lord sustains me.

You are cared for and kept safe.
You can call to Him and He gives you strength.
Your life is held in place because of His power.
He will lift the weight of shame and exhaustion
from you. He gives you rest because you
depend on Him and not on yourself.

HE IS

YOUR CREATOR

PSALM 24:1

The earth is the Lord's,
and everything in it, the world, and all who live in it.

God is in control of the world.
He has not lost His authority.
You serve the powerful Creator of all things.
All things are known by Him and
are under His dominion. Be comforted
knowing He knows and loves you.

HE SPEAKS
TO YOU

PSALM 25:14

The Lord confides
in those who fear Him;
He makes His covenant known to them.

He will give you wisdom as you know Him
better. He desires you to seek Him.
He will show you His faithfulness
and His power as you spend time with Him.
He is personal and longs for your heart
to be tender toward Him.

HE IS YOUR
SALVATION
PSALM 27:1

The Lord is my light
and my salvation—whom shall I fear? The Lord is the
stronghold of my life—of whom shall I be afraid?

You don't have to be fearful.
The God of the Universe will protect you.
When things don't make sense, trust Him.
When you have been wronged,
know that He is doing something bigger
that you can't see.

HE STRENGTHENS
YOU

PSALM 29:11

The Lord gives strength to His people;
the Lord blesses His people with peace.

He fills you with the endurance you need.

He enables you to face whatever

difficulties come into your life.

He will give you a restful heart —not for

your glory, but for His.

HE
PROTECTS YOU

PSALM 32:7

You are my hiding place;
You will protect me from trouble
and surround me with songs of deliverance.

You can walk boldly through your day
knowing He is your defender. Your identity
is found in Him. He says, "You are mine!"
Remember "whose you are."
He is fighting on your behalf.

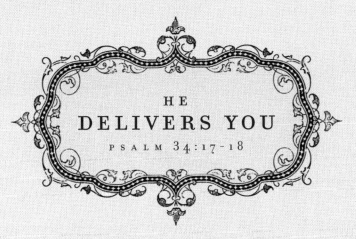

HE
DELIVERS YOU
PSALM 34:17-18

The righteous cry out,
and the Lord hears them; He delivers them from all
their troubles. The Lord is close to the brokenhearted
and saves those who are crushed in spirit.

The Father hears your cries of sadness.
Your brokenness is known to Him.
Remember, you are not alone.
There is hope as you keep your eyes on Him
instead of on your circumstances.
He is your deliverer.

HE IS
MAJESTIC
PSALM 36:5-6A

Your love, O Lord,
reaches to the heavens, Your faithfulness to the skies.
Your righteousness is like the mighty mountains,
Your justice like the great deep.

His love for you is beyond your
understanding. He longs to show you His
majesty. Turn your eyes to see the beauty
and glory of His creation.
Ponder the vastness of His abilities.

HE IS
GRACIOUS
PSALM 145:8

The Lord is gracious
and compassionate, slow to anger
and rich in love.

He is not in a hurry.
No matter what you've done, He patiently
waits for you. He is interested in the
condition of your heart. Take His hand
and let Him take your burden.

PRESERVES YOU

PSALM 138:7

Though I walk in the midst of trouble,
You preserve my life; You stretch out Your hand
against the anger of my foes,
with Your right hand You save me

God sees the dangers around you
and the reasons you become anxious.
He is fighting for you. He offers
His strong arm for you to cling to. You can walk
in peace, even in the chaos of this world.

HE IS
TRUSTWORTHY
PSALM 84:12

O Lord Almighty,
blessed is the man who trusts in You.

As frustrations occur, you can trust Him.

You can say, "Your will, not mine."

He brings the blessing of rest and peace,

as you submit to Him.

He is the Lord Almighty and you are

cared for by Him.

HE IS
POWERFUL
PSALM 89:11

The heavens are Yours,
and Yours also the earth;
You founded the world and all that is in it.

He is over all! Nothing is out of His control.

He holds all things in His hands.

You can rest and move forward with joy.

Don't be fearful.

Trust in Him and His mighty power.

HE IS YOUR
REFUGE

PSALM 91:1-2

He who dwells in the shelter
of the Most High will rest in the shadow of the Almighty.
I will say of the LORD, "He is my refuge
and my fortress, my God, in whom I trust."

During your day, if you will go often into His presence, you can relax your mind. Being with Him equals peace. You can let go of "figuring it all out" or "getting it all right." He is trustworthy and able.

HE IS YOUR
GUIDE

PSALM 73:23-24

Yet I am always with You;
You hold me by my right hand. You guide me with Your
counsel, and afterward You will take me into glory.

You are not alone. Your spirit can be free
knowing He holds your hand.
He provides you with everything you need
to make decisions. He gives clarity to your
clouded mind. One day, you will see Him face
to face in heaven.

HE IS YOUR
PORTION
PSALM 73:26

My flesh and my heart may fail,
but God is the strength
of my heart and my portion forever.

Yes, at times you feel like giving up and giving
in. But don't lose hope.
Let Him be strong for you. He will help you
endure, even in your weakness.

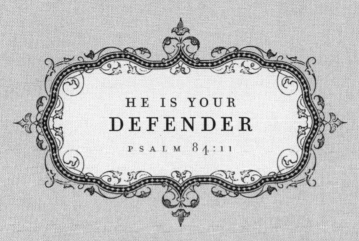

HE IS YOUR
DEFENDER

PSALM 84:11

For the Lord God is a sun and shield;
the Lord bestows favor and honor; no good thing
does He withhold from those whose walk is blameless.

He will show you His mercy. He is your
defender. He knows what you need at every
moment and He will provide.
Your flesh may not think it's enough,
but God is your life sustainer.

HE
FORGIVES
PSALM 85:2-3

You forgave the iniquity of Your people
and covered all their sins. You set aside
all Your wrath and turned from Your fierce anger.

He is righteous and declares you righteous.

He is forgiving and you are forgiven.

He doesn't give you what you deserve;

He is full of grace and mercy. His kindness is

unending! All praises to Him!

HE IS YOUR
HOPE

PSALM 119:81

My soul faints with longing
for Your salvation, but I have put my hope in Your Word.

His Word is the hope of your life.

Your flesh and mind can lie to you.

You can become exhausted and lose hope when
you look around.

It is only His Word that brings springs of life.

Go only to Him for your comfort!

HE MAKES YOU
FREE
PSALM 118:5-6

In my anguish I cried to the Lord,
and He answered by setting me free. The Lord is with me;
I will not be afraid. What can man do to me?

He sets you free! It is Him that you trust.
The world is at His feet and He guards you.
Yes, life is painful, and yes, He is working.
He will bring freedom
to your captive heart and mind!

HE IS
MIGHTY
PSALM 145:3-4

Great is the Lord
and most worthy of praise; His greatness no one
can fathom. One generation will commend Your works
to another; they will tell of Your mighty acts.

Praise Him because He is worthy.
The world can't begin to understand how
mighty He is. Speak this to your friends and
children. Proclaim the miracles and the
faithfulness you have seen. Great is the Lord!

HE GUARDS
YOU
PSALM 139:5-6

You hem me in—behind and before;
You have laid Your hand upon me. Such knowledge
is too wonderful for me, too lofty for me to attain.

He goes out before you, covers you on all sides,
and follows behind you.
You are like a button in a button hole—held in
place, surrounded by His presence.
What beautiful news! Meditate on this truth
and experience great peace!

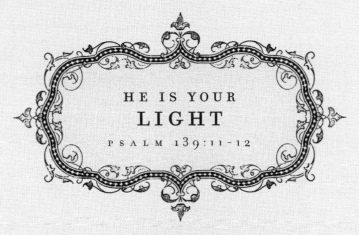

HE IS YOUR
LIGHT
PSALM 139:11-12

If I say,

"Surely the darkness will hide me and the light become
night around me," even the darkness
will not be dark to You; the night will shine like the day,
for darkness is as light to You.

He is always there. He never sleeps or gets
tired. The night and the day are the same to
Him. You can be frail and fearful.
but He is powerful and rules all things.
He is always available, always watching,
always an ever ready power source.

HE FORGIVES
YOU
PSALM 130:3-4

If You, O Lord, kept a record of sins,
O Lord, who could stand? But with You
there is forgiveness; therefore you are feared.

You need Him! The flesh is bent toward sin
and sadness. The flesh wants to build a
reputation for itself. God is mindful of the
flesh's condition and desires to bring healing.
He is to be honored and adored
for His great mercy!

HE BRINGS
PEACE
PSALM 127:1

Unless the Lord builds the house,
its builders labor in vain. Unless the Lord watches over
the city, the watchmen stand guard in vain.

Welcome Him into your family, marriage, and
life. Look to His Word for how to live.
Wait for Him to bring the wisdom that you
need. He can bring strength, order, and peace
to you life. Be willing to hear from Him and
prepare for change!

HE IS YOUR
SHADE
PSALM 121:5-8

The Lord watches over you—
the Lord is your shade at your right hand; the sun will
not harm you by day, nor the moon by night. The Lord
will keep you from all harm—He will watch over your
life; the Lord will watch over your coming and going
both now and forevermore.

Thank Him for His amazing blessings to you.
He brings good things into your life.
He cares for you in all you do. Seek Him and
keep looking for the holy work He is doing
behind the scenes in your life!

HE LIFTS
YOU UP

PSALM 40:1-2

I waited patiently for the Lord;
He turned to me and heard my cry. He lifted me out
of the slimy pit, out of the mud and mire; He set my feet
on a rock and gave me a firm place to stand.

Oh, His faithfulness is amazing!
His watchful eye is on you and He is listening
for your prayer. You are not forgotten
or lost. Your inability to see "the big picture"
is okay. He will give you perspective, wisdom,
and clarity—it's not trouble for Him!

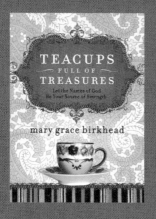
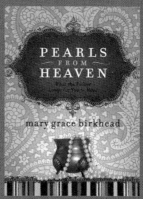

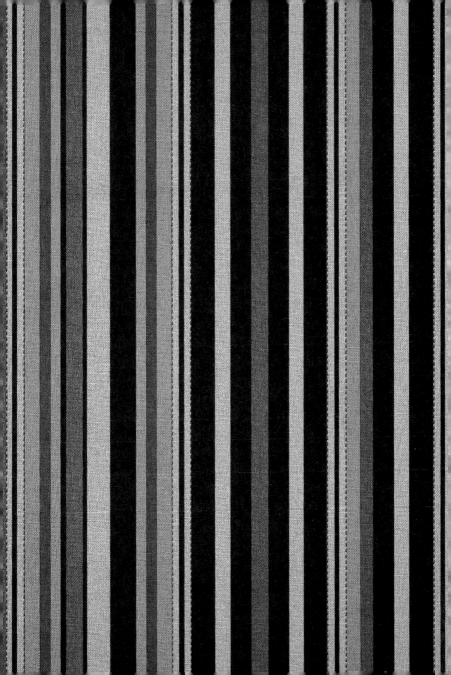